Migration-Induced HIV and AIDS in Rural Mozambique and Swaziland

Jonathan Crush, Ines Raimundo, Hamilton Simelane, Boaventura Cau and David Dorey

Series Editor:
Prof. Jonathan Crush

Southern African Migration Programme (SAMP)
International Organization for Migration (IOM)
2010

ACKNOWLEDGEMENTS

We wish to thank the PHAMSA Program of the IOM (Pretoria) for funding the research on which this report is based. The survey was designed by a working group which included Mark Lurie, Krista House, David Dorey and Hamilton Simelane. Brian Williams alerted us to some important work in this area. We would like to thank all these colleagues for their input and assistance. Ashley Hill assisted with data analysis and report writing. Cassandra Eberhardt, Barbara Rijks, Maria Salamone, Katy Barwise and Searle Schonewille assisted with editing. We would also like to thank the IDRC for its support of SAMP and the DFID for funding the publication of this report.

Published by Idasa, 6 Spin Street, Church Square, Cape Town, 8001, and Southern African Research Centre, Queen's University, Canada.

ISBN 978-1-920409-49-4
First published 2010
Design by Bronwen Müller

Bound and printed by Logo Print, Cape Town

Contents

Page

Tables

Page

Figures — Page

EXECUTIVE SUMMARY

South Africa's gold mining workforce has the highest prevalence rates of tuberculosis and HIV infection of any industrial sector in the country. The contract migrant labour system, which has long outlived apartheid, is responsible for this unacceptable situation. The spread of HIV to rural communities in Southern Africa is not well understood. The accepted wisdom is that migrants leave for the mines, engage in high-risk behaviour, contract the virus and return to infect their rural partners. This model fails to deal with the phenomenon of rural-rural transmission and cases of HIV discordance (when the female migrant is infected and the male migrant not). Nor does it reveal whether all rural partners are equally at risk of infection.

This study examines the vulnerability of rural partners in southern Mozambique and southern Swaziland, which are two major source areas for migrant miners. It presents the results of surveys with miners and partners in these two sending-areas and affords the opportunity to compare two different mine-sending areas. The two areas are not only geographically and culturally different, they have had contrasting experiences with the mine labour system over the last two decades. The spread of HIV in Southern Africa in the 1990s coincided with major downsizing and retrenchment in the gold mining industry which impacted differently on Mozambique and Swaziland. Swaziland has been in decline as a source of mine migrants while Mozambique remained a relatively stable source of mine migrants. The study therefore aims not only to shed light on vulnerability in mine sending areas, but also to draw out any contrasts that might exist between two mine-sending areas that were inserted into the mine migrant labour system in different ways during the expansion of the HIV epidemic.

The surveys collected data on (a) the age and socio-economic profiles of miners and partners; (b) migration behaviour (particularly how often migrants returned home and for how long; (c) the knowledge of and attitudes towards HIV and AIDS among both groups; (d) sexual behaviour and protection measures against infection and (e) perceptions of vulnerability and risk. Knowledge of HIV and AIDS is reasonably good amongst residents of both areas. Many of the common myths about HIV are held by only a tiny minority. Most seem to know what puts them at risk, know that the disease is fatal, know that ART is not a remedy and do not appear to have a great deal of faith in traditional healers. One exception is the rather large proportion of Mozambican miners who believe the disease is curable. If anything, rural partners are better informed than miners. In both Mozambique and Swaziland, the main source of knowledge is not workplace programmes on the mines or in the community nor peer education nor the medical community, but radio.

Perception of personal vulnerability is also high. Yet, both miners and female rural partners of migrants are at risk through their behaviour. The reasons, though, are quite different. In the case of miners, high risk behaviour is a consequence of the migrant labour system which sees them spend the greater part of the working year away from home in an all-male environment of macho masculinity with easy access to transactional sex. These miners are aware that condom use would reduce their risk of contracting HIV but actual use is sporadic to non-existent. Condom use is rejected on grounds of personal preference or attributed to forgetfulness.

Miners at home are even less likely to use condoms than when they are on the mine. The risks of contracting HIV are certainly lower (since commercial sex workers on the mines exhibit much higher HIV prevalence than rural partners). But their unwillingness to use protection puts their rural partners at greatly increased risk. Rural partners perceive themselves to be at high risk precisely because their partners do not wish to use protection. Miners clearly expect their partners to be faithful and do not see themselves at risk when they go home. Any woman who insists on condom use is seen to be implicitly questioning her partner's fidelity. Women's lack of use of condoms has virtually nothing to do with personal preference. Partners of migrant miners wish to use condoms to protect themselves. Their inability to do so with the frequency and consistency that they would like is related to the demands of men for unprotected sex. Ultimately, therefore, it is the gendered relations of inequality that make it very difficult for women to protect themselves against the high-risk environment of the mines.

One of the basic hypotheses of this study was that different migration patterns affect the risk profile of miners and rural partners. Mozambican miners return home only once a year for annual leave. Swazi miners, in contrast, visit home at least once a month or every month or two. Yet, both engage in equally risky behaviour while they are away at work. This places Swazi women at greater personal risk than their Mozambican counterparts.

On the other hand, the comparison between Mozambican and Swazi women suggests that the Mozambican partners may be more prone to forming other relationships outside their primary relationship with their usually absent partner for a host of different reasons including emotional and financial support. In some cases, increased poverty from a reduced flow of remittances may force some rural women to seek support through other relationships.

INTRODUCTION

South Africa's gold mining workforce has the highest prevalence rates of HIV and TB infection of any industrial sector in the country.[1] In the late 1980s, HIV prevalence amongst migrant miners was less than 1%.[2] Only ten years later, it was over 25% and still climbing.[3] HIV infection, in turn, dramatically increases vulnerability to TB. TB prevalence increased from 806 per 100,000 in 1991 to 3,821 per 100,000 in 2004 to over 7,000 per 100,000 in 2009.[4] The contract migrant labour system, which has long outlived apartheid, is responsible for this situation.[5] Absence from home, a culture of macho male sexuality on the mines, the ready availability of casual and commercial sex, and the constant fear and personal experience of death and dismemberment underground, all place miners at very high risk of HIV infection.[6]

The intimate connection between migration and infectious disease pre-dates the advent of HIV and AIDS. Indeed, it as old as the migrant labour system itself. Since the beginning of South Africa's gold mining industry in the late nineteenth century, labour migration has impacted on the health of migrant miners and their rural partners in South Africa and neighbouring countries.[7] Particularly devastating were the lung and infectious diseases (such as STIs and TB), that accompanied poor working conditions and long periods of separation and relationship disruption. In the words of Shula Marks, pre-existing patterns of oscillating labour migration in Southern Africa rendered HIV and AIDS an "epidemic waiting to happen."[8]

Although there is now a large literature on the vulnerability of male migrant workers to HIV, the relationship between migration and the spread of HIV to rural communities is imperfectly understood.[9] The conventional wisdom is captured in a somewhat one-dimensional model: migrants leave for the mines, engage in high-risk behaviour, contract the virus and return to infect their unprotected rural partners. In the case of Mozambique, for example, Collins argues that the higher rate of HIV prevalence in the centre and south (compared to other parts of the country) is directly related to the influence of migrant labour to the South African mines: "Rising prevalence levels in this region in part reflect increased commercial and migrant mineworker travel south since the 1992 peace agreement. An estimated 50,000 Mozambicans, most from the southern and central regions, currently work in South African mines, where HIV rates are very high. Many of them return home on annual leave infected with HIV and infect their wives."[10] According to this model, the virus spreads to rural areas purely by infected male migrants returning home and infecting their partners. Darrell Roodt's 2004 award-winning movie *Yesterday* is a classic representation of this model, accompanied (for dramatic effect) by the stigmatization and expulsion of the migrant and his female partner from the rural community.[11]

Recent research undertaken in migrant-sending areas in the KwaZulu Natal province of South Africa challenges this model of transmission from migrants to rural partners.[12] The study compared "migrant couples" (in which at least one of the partners migrated for work) to "non-migrant couples" and found that the former were more likely to have one or both partners infected with HIV (35% versus 19%). These couples were also more likely to be HIV discordant (27% versus 15%) i.e. one partner is infected and the other not. However, the research also showed that amongst couples in which only one partner was infected, in nearly a third of cases (30%) the migrant was actually HIV-negative and the rural partner was HIV positive. Clearly, an HIV-positive woman whose migrant spouse is not infected must have been infected by someone else. This suggests that a more nuanced understanding is needed of the risk behaviours of both migrants and their rural partners and the responses required to reduce personal vulnerability to infection.

In practice, there are many mediating factors affecting the vulnerability of female partners to infection by a male migrant.These include the recency and acuteness of male infection, his viral load, the presence of genital ulceration, herpes simplex virus-2 positivity, concurrency, male circumcision and age.[13] Coffee *et al* have modeled the impact of migration on the HIV epidemic using data from Kwazulu-Natal and find that migration primarily influences the spread of HIV by increasing high-risk behaviour, rather than by connecting areas of low and high risk.[14] The model also predicts that if migration is accompanied by increased sexual risk behaviour by migrant men, HIV prevalence among female partners increases tenfold. In contrast, if migration occurs infrequently, the predicted epidemic would be only one fifth of that currently observed. For a given level of high risk behaviour by migrants, the frequency of return home would also dramatically affect the risk of contracting HIV by rural partners. Another critical factor impacting on the vulnerability of rural partners is the nature of gender relations between men and women in the rural migrant sending areas. Amongst other things, this influences the degree to which, and with what consequences, rural women can take measures to protect themselves against infection.

The spread of HIV in Southern Africa in the 1990s coincided with major downsizing and retrenchment in the mining industry. The South African gold mines lost over 150,000 jobs after 1990 (with employment levels dropping from 406,000 in 1990 to 230,000 in 2004). To the extent that migrants were precluded from working any longer on the mines, they and their partners became less vulnerable to infection since they were no longer exposed to high-risk situations on the mines. These massive job losses profoundly impacted on migrant-sending communities and exacerbated already high levels of unemployment.[15]

The new economic reality forced a number of women to enter the workforce and engage in forms of cross-border trade to supplement household income. As a result, the female members of the households of former mine migrants themselves potentially became more vulnerable to HIV as the conditions in which they lived and worked in cities and on farms increased their vulnerability.

In order to examine the vulnerability to HIV infection of rural partners, two contrasting mine migrant sending areas were chosen for this study: southern Mozambique and southern Swaziland. The two areas are not only geographically and culturally different, they have had contrasting experiences with the mine labour system over the last two decades. One (Swaziland) has been in decline as a source of mine migrants; the other (Mozambique) has been a relatively stable source of mine migrants. The study therefore aims not only to shed light on the parameters of vulnerability in mine sending areas, but also to draw out any contrasts that might exist between two mine-sending areas that have been inserted into the mine migrant labour system in different ways at the height of the HIV epidemic.

MINE LABOUR FROM MOZAMBIQUE AND SWAZILAND

DOWNSIZING THE WORKFORCE

For many decades, southern Mozambique and southern Swaziland have been major source areas for male migrant workers on the South African gold mines.[16] The numbers from Mozambique rose steadily in the decades after 1920, peaking at just over 100,000 in 1960 (Table 1). The numbers from Swaziland were always lower (though comparable in terms of the proportion of the population) and peaked much later (in 1990). The sudden drop in Mozambique between 1975 and 1980 came right after independence. Fearing that the new socialist government would withdraw all Mozambican miners, the mining companies quickly sought out new sources of labour. Swaziland was one of the beneficiaries as the number of Swazi miners doubled between 1975 and 1990.

Table 1: Mine Migration to South Africa, 1920-2005		
Year	Mozambique	Swaziland
1920	77,921	3,449
1925	73,210	3,999
1930	77,828	4,345
1935	62,576	6,865
1940	74,693	7,152
1945	78,588	5,688
1950	86,246	6,619
1955	99,449	6,682
1960	101,733	6,623
1965	89,191	5,580
1970	93,203	6,269
1975	97,216	8,391
1980	39,539	8,090
1985	50,126	12,365
1990	43,951	16,618
1995	53,321	14,611
2000	44,245	8,079
2005	46,256	6,878
Source: Crush, Jeeves and Yudelman, South Africa's Labor Empire; TEBA.		

When HIV arrived on the mines in the late 1980s, the number of Swazi miners was over 40% of the number of Mozambicans. However, this scenario changed very quickly in the 1990s. Swaziland experienced major downsizing of its mine workforce while Mozambique did not. As Figure 1 shows, although the number of Mozambican miners fluctuated during the 1990s, there were more in 2003 than there had been in 1990. Over the same time period, the mine workforce from Swaziland was cut in half. By 2007, the number of Swazi miners was only 20% of the number of Mozambican miners.

The reasons for this change in recruiting patterns in the 1990s have never been properly explained. The rate of Swazi retrenchments was comparable to that in Lesotho, Botswana and South Africa itself. So the question is really why Mozambique did not experience a similar decline and why the proportion of Mozambicans in the workforce increased from 10% to 25% over the course of the decade. One possible explanation is that Mozambicans were not well-represented on the mines that suffered most lay-offs. Another is that Mozambican miners were less militant than their South African counterparts and were therefore preferred by employers. However, general levels of militancy on the mines declined amongst all mineworkers after 1990. It is likely that the HIV and AIDS epidemic also played a role. Mine managers would have quickly realised that HIV prevalence was lower in Mozambique than in other sources areas like Swaziland and Lesotho. As miners were retrenched, it would have made sense to mine managers to recruit any new workers from a region with much lower general rates of infection. And that really only meant Mozambique.

Figure 1: Migrant Labour on South African Mines, 1990-2007

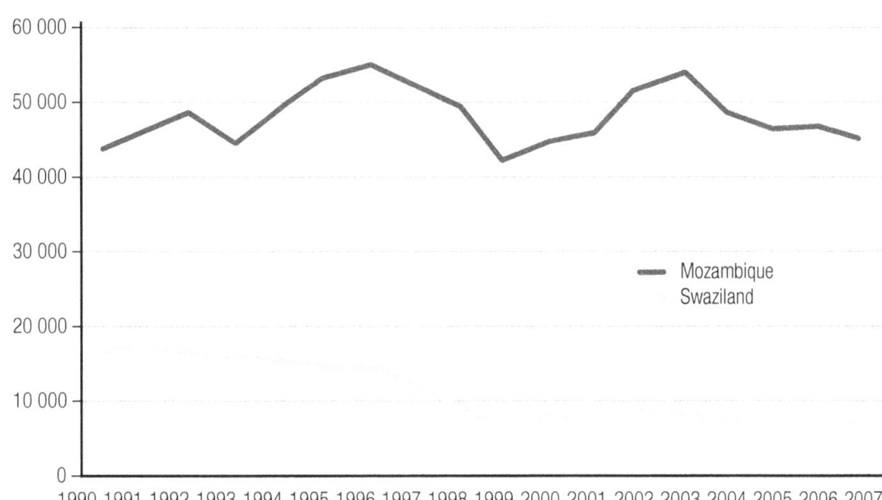

HIV/AIDS AND THE CHANGING AGE PROFILE OF MIGRANT MINERS

Declining employment opportunities for migrants in the post-1990 mining industry meant that the average age of those who remained began to rise. A 1997 SAMP survey of Mozambican miners found that only 5% were under the age of 35 while 61% were over the age of 45.[17] Another SAMP survey only eight years later showed a dramatic change in the age composition of the Mozambican mine workforce. Now 39% were under the age of 35 and only 29% were over the age of 45. The most plausible explanation for this dramatic shift in age profile is HIV and AIDS.

Older miners were getting too sick to work or dying of AIDS and they were being replaced by younger, HIV negative, men from rural Mozambique. A key question (which this paper sets out to answer) is whether these miners, who joined the industry in a period of heightened awareness about HIV and AIDS, are less susceptible to infection than the previous generation. After 2002, the number of miners recruited from Mozambique began to decline (from 52,000 in 2003 to 45,000 in 2007). The reason could be the undoubted political pressure to hire South Africans (something the mines had successfully resisted for decades) or it could be that with rates of HIV on the rise in rural Mozambique, a long-standing competitive advantage of Mozambique came to an end.

Table 2: Age of Migrant Miners from Mozambique and Swaziland			
Age of Miners	Mozambique (1997) (%)	Mozambique (2005) (%)	Swaziland (2005) (%)
<35	5	39	19
35-39	10	18	28
40-44	24	14	25
45-49	39	9	16
50-54	14	11	7
55-59	6	7	4
>60	2	2	1
Source: SAMP Surveys			

Age data for miners from Swaziland is only available for 2005. What this suggests is that there has been little 'new blood' from Swaziland for some time (with only 19% under 35 compared with Mozambique's 39%).

MOBILITY AND VULNERABILITY

The 2005 SAMP Survey revealed dramatic differences in the frequency of home visits by miners from Mozambique and Swaziland. In the case of Mozambique, two thirds of miners returned only once or twice a year and another 21% less than once a year. In contrast, nearly half of the Swazi migrants returned home at least once a month and another 37% at least once every three months. Only 13% returned once or twice a year. Around 87% of miners in both countries are married or cohabiting.

Table 3: Frequency of Return Home By Migrant Miners		
	Mozambique (%)	Swaziland (%)
> Twice a Month	2	7
Once a Month	2	41
> Twice in Three Months	1	19
Once Every Three Months	9	18
Once Every Six Months	29	7
Once a Year	37	6
Less Than Once A Year	21	2

Epidemiologists have shown that the probability of HIV infection within an HIV discordant couple is related to the frequency of sexual intercourse. In general,the risk of HIV infection for rural women increases with the frequency of sexual relations with their migrant partners. In the context of a migrant labour system, frequency is partly a function of how often partners are able to see one another. The frequency with which miners return home is therefore a general surrogate measure of the degree of risk of infection for their partners. Holding all other factors equal, the risk of HIV infection from unprotected sex is clearly much higher amongst rural partners in Swaziland than in Mozambique.

HIV AND AIDS IN RURAL SWAZILAND AND MOZAMBIQUE

SWAZILAND: FULL-BLOWN AIDS

The first reported case of AIDS in Swaziland was in 1987. Today, it has one of the highest rates of HIV infection in the world. In 1992, the first ante-natal clinic (ANC) survey was carried out and showed an HIV prevalence of 3.9%. In 1994, prevalence had jumped to 16.1% and in 2002 to 38.5%.[18] By 2004, the rate had jumped again to 42.6% (Figure 2).[19] Rates of HIV infection are highest among women of child-bearing age in their 20s and 30s. The impact of the epidemic is being felt throughout the country. The death rate increased from 11 to 20 per 1000 population between 1997 and 2003 and the infant mortality rate increased from 88 to 109 per 1000 over the same time period. Life expectancy has fallen to 40 for males and 41 for females.[20]

Figure 2: HIV Prevalence (ANC Respondents), 1992-2004

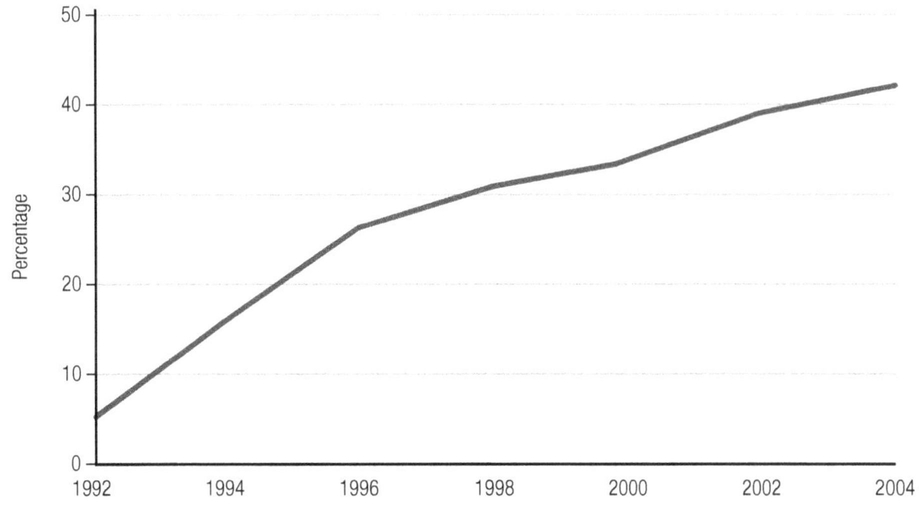

The dramatic spread of HIV in Swaziland has been attributed to high levels of internal mobility and cross-border migration to South Africa. Whiteside, for example, argues that the people of Swaziland are "extremely mobile" within the country and, in addition, "there is considerable cross border mobility, particularly to South Africa."[21] He draws particular attention to migrant miners who "travel as single men for periods of up to a year."[22] In fact, though their employment contracts are a year long, Swazi migrants return home quite frequently during the year. This only magnifies the vulnerability of their rural partners.

After the end of apartheid, cross-border movement between Swaziland and South Africa increased dramatically. Legal border crossings from Swaziland to South Africa grew from under 200,000 in 1991 to over 800,000 in 2003.[23] While mobility is widely said to increase vulnerability to HIV, different forms and frequencies of movement impact differently on vulnerability.[24] With regard to Swazi miners, Whiteside argues that the vulnerability of Swazi miners is attributable to anonymity, loneliness, an inability to maintain stable relationships and an environment where life is cheap.[25] These increase the likelihood of non-regular sex and sexually transmitted infections. The mine environment also generates a machismo culture conducive to sexual behaviours that put miners at considerable risk.[26]

ANC HIV prevalence rates in the southern Shiselweni District (where this research took place) are comparable to those in the other three districts of the country (Table 4). As Whiteside points out, the epidemic is "uniformly bad" in Swaziland with little difference between rural and urban areas and between districts.[27] Others have argued that although Shiselweni does not have the highest HIV prevalence, it does have the highest number of AIDS-related deaths.[28] This they attribute to the greater incidence of poverty and migration patterns out of Shiselweni. The 1997 Swaziland Census showed that Shiselweni District had the highest rate of out-migration with 90% of migrants moving internally to Manzini.[29] In other words, many Shiselweni residents with HIV are living and working in Manzini, pushing up that region's prevalence rate. At the same time, people with full-blown AIDS who can no longer work invariably return to their home Shiselweni region to die. As mine migrants with HIV become ill and are unable to work on the mines, they too return to Shiselweni.

Table 4: HIV Infection Trends Among ANC Respondents by District, 1994-2002					
Region	1994	1996	1998	2000	2002
Hhohho	15.5	26.3	30.3	32.3	36.6
Lubombo	16.8	26.5	31.5	34.5	38.5
Manzini	15.6	27.7	34.8	41	41.2
Shiselweni	16.8	23.9	29.6	27	37.9
Source: Whiteside, 2003, p. 15.					

MOZAMBIQUE: HIV RISING

After a slower start, HIV is now spreading rapidly in rural Mozambique. In 2004, the national infection rate was estimated at 16.2%. An estimated 500 new infections occur each day.[30] As in the rest of the region, the HIV epidemic in Mozambique has particularly affected women. The prevalence rate for young women between the ages of 15 and 19 is twice that of young men. Women between 20 and 24 are four times more likely to have HIV than their male peers.[31] As Table 5 shows, rates in the North are much lower than in the Centre and South.[32]

Table 5: Estimated Adult HIV Prevalence Rates, Mozambique, 2002			
Region	Province	Prevalence Rates	
		Provincial %	Regional %
South	MaputoCity	13	13.2
	Maputo Province	14.3	
	Gaza	16	
	Inhambane	9.6	
Centre	Sofala	18.7	16.5
	Manica	21.1	
	Tete	19.8	
	Zambezia	12.7	
North	Nampula	5.2	5.7
	Niassa	6.8	
	Cabo Delgado	6.4	
Mozambique National			12.2
Sources: Ministry of Health (2002) and Ministry of Health et al. (2001), based on observations from 20 health posts, some of them rural (Arndt 2003: 2)			

Regional differences in HIV prevalence have been related to internal and external population movements.[33] Beckmann and Rai, for example, argue that a number of overlapping mobility-related factors are responsible for the rapid spread of HIV in Mozambique:

> The epidemic has been fuelled by the return of refugees from neighbouring countries, the introduction of peacekeeping forces from high-prevalence countries, and a marked increase in cross-border trade. The impact of the movement of troops from West Africa is thought to be part of the cause of the spread of HIV-2 in Mozambique, as military personnel have higher prevalence rates and tend to exhibit risky behaviour. The railway line that passes by Gaza links Mozambique with South Africa and Zimbabwe. During the war in the 1980s, the trains transporting relief food were guarded by soldiers from the latter countries. As a result of the dire conditions, prostitution increased in that region. In southern Mozambique, miners with relatively high wages meet the staggering poverty of rural women struggling to make a living. This combination of poverty and inequality greatly favours the spread of HIV.[34]

A 2002 UNESCO study suggested that a number of socio-cultural factors were also facilitating the spread of HIV: initiation rites, polygamous marriages, religious practices, death rites, taboos, witchcraft and commercial sex.[35]

Access to health care in rural Mozambique is particularly poor. Less than 40% of the population has access to basic services. Poor transportation and communications infrastructure mean that many areas of the country cannot access services when needed. Beckman and Rai found that the services that are provided in Mozambique are often inadequate and provide questionable information and educational services.[36] They conclude, "the level of knowledge of AIDS is very low in all ranks of health-care workers. Most health workers are unable to provide complete information to patients and are not trained to treat opportunistic infections."[37]

STUDY METHODOLOGY

The primary objective of the research was to examine the vulnerability to HIV and AIDS of the rural partners of migrant miners. This population has been largely ignored in the existing literature on the mining sector which tends to focus on mineworkers themselves and their vulnerability at the place of work. The research was planned by a SAMP working group which first developed and tested a common questionnaire for use in both sites. As the project developed, it became clear that the vulnerability of rural women was intimately connected both to their own material and social circumstances and to the behaviours and attitudes of their migrant partners.

Hence, a twin focus developed on migrant miners (who were all interviewed while at home) and their rural partners. Not only did this approach provide insights into the vulnerability of the rural partners, it also provided an opportunity to make comparisons between the behaviour and attitudes of the two groups. In other words, the research permitted two axes of comparison: first, between two different mine-sending areas, and second, between migrant men and their rural partners.

The vast majority of Mozambican mine migrants come from the south of the country.[38] Approximately 40% of miners are from Gaza Province, 28% from Inhambane and 27% from Maputo. A SAMP study in the late 1990s showed that within Gaza Province, 27% of miners were from Xai Xai District, 21% from Chokwe District, 20% from Chibuto, 15% from Manjacaze and 9% from Bilene/Macia.[39] The area in Mozambique chosen for the study was the Chokwe District of Gaza Province (Figure 3). The district was selected because of its well-established historical ties to mine migration to South Africa and its contemporary importance as a mine-sending area.[40] At the time of the survey, Chokwe District supplied approximately 4,000 miners to the South African mines, second in importance only to Xai Xai. The HIV prevalence rate for the Chokwe District was estimated by the Ministry of Health to be 22% of all adults in 2003.[41] The interviews were conducted in three communities within the District: Chilembene, Macarretane and the regional capital of Chokwe itself.

Figure 3: Gaza Province and Chokwe District, Mozambique

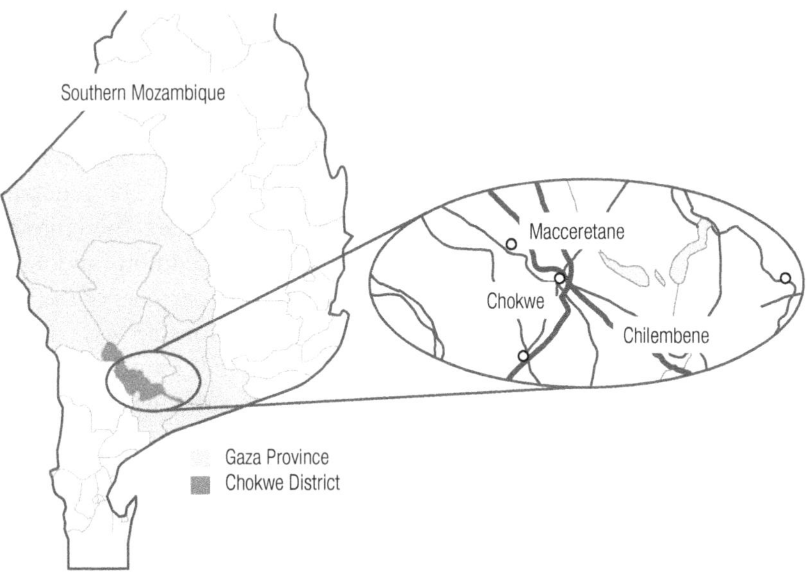

In the case of Swaziland, the Shiselweni District in the south of the country has always supplied a disproportionate number of migrant miners.[42] The research was conducted in several different rural parts of the District (Figure 4).

Figure 4: Shiselweni District, Swaziland

The questionnaire was administered to a total of 50 working male miners and 98 rural female partners in Swaziland and 40 miners and 80 rural partners in Mozambique. Snowball sampling techniques were used to identify interviewees. However, comparison with the more larger and more systematic SAMP sample in 2005 suggests that the miners are broadly representative of their respective national cohorts. No such control group exists with regard to the rural partners. The generalizability of the findings, particularly with regard to partners, therefore need to be carefully qualified. These are studies of a limited non-random sample. The women interviewed were not the actual partners of the miners interviewed. To interview both partners in a relationship was considered to be less likely to elicit honest responses. In addition, the survey primarily posed questions about attitudes, perceptions, knowledge and behaviour. The results are likely to be more reliable about awareness and perceptions of risk than self-reported sexual activity.

PROFILE OF RESPONDENTS

SWAZILAND

The majority of mineworkers interviewed were in their forties while the rural female partners were mainly in their thirties. Both groups were also relatively uneducated, the majority not having gone beyond primary school. Nearly three quarters of male migrants were married (72%) and another 10% were co-habiting. Only 2 of the miners interviewed were single. Most migrant miners therefore have long-term relationships with rural women. They are not, as they were in the past, young, single men.

Swazi migrant miners earn relatively low incomes. The average wage of respondents was only R2,000 per month.[43] The amount is small but still higher than the average monthly wage in Swaziland. Almost 80% of migrant-sending households had no other source of income than the remittances sent home by the miners. The money is used to support very large families: 45% of the men interviewed support between five and nine children, while a further 22% support ten children or more. Only 5% had no children to support. The majority of mine migrants support between one and four adults in addition to the children. These are large families if we consider that according to the Swaziland Census in 1997 the average family size in the country was roughly five. Clearly, the AIDS epidemic has dramatically increased the number of dependants supported by migrants.

The migrants work at several different mines in South Africa, the majority at West Deep Level and Vaal Reefs. Most have worked in the industry for more than eight years, which is consistent with the general pattern in the mining industry of a stable, but aging, workforce. Many are machine operators (over 40%), with the remainder being general labourers and drivers. Swazi miners are generally known for their specialization in operating mine machinery. The majority of the mine migrants are accommodated in single-sex mine compounds. Some, however, rent accommodation in neighbouring communities. According to some informants, this is especially true of migrants who have forged extramarital relationships with women in the vicinity of the mine irrespective of whether they have wives or girlfriends back in Swaziland.

Most of the Swazi migrants return regularly to their rural homes. Around 60% visit their homes in Swaziland monthly, while 30% said they do so every other month. This was corroborated by the rural female partners; just over half (52%) said that they see their husbands monthly. Regardless of the intervals between visits, the length of each visit home is usually short. The majority (around 60%) said that their home visits last for 1-2 days. Another 30% said that their visits typically last for 3-5 days. As many as 40% of the migrant mineworkers are sometimes visited by their partners at the mines.

MOZAMBIQUE

The Mozambican minerswere also relatively uneducated. Around 70% had only completed primary schooling. Some 15% had not been to school at all. Only one of the miners was single while the remainder were either married (50%) or cohabitating (48%). More of the rural partners (61%) said they were co-habiting while only a third (32%) were formally married. Five of the partners were widows. All of the miners have large numbers of dependants, with the average supporting nine other people. Of these, 5 are children and 4 are adults. Five of the miners said they had 15 or more dependants.

Rural partners are heavily dependent on migrant miners for income. The majority (74%) said they earned less than 1,000,000 Mts per month and therefore contribute little to household income (Table 6). Ninety percent listed their occupation as camponesa (rural agriculturalist). Most miners earn over 3,000,000 Mts (135 USD) per month. These findings are confirmed by other studies on remittances which show that remitted funds and goods are integral to household income and survival in migrant-sending Mozambique.[44] The death or disability of a miner therefore has very serious ramifications for the rural household. The number of people affected will also be large, given the size of most mine migrant-sending households.

Table 6: Average Monthly Income for Miners and Partners

Income level (Mts)	Male Miners		Female Partners	
	No.	%	No.	%
Less than 500,000 (23 USD)	5	12	45	56
500,000 to 1,000,000	2	5	14	17
1,000,001 to 1,500,000	4	10	6	8
1,500,001 to 2,000,000	0	0	3	5
2,000,001 to 2,500,000	0	0	2	2
2,500,001 to 3,000,000	3	8	1	1
More than 3,000,000 (135 USD)	24	60	2	2
Don't know	2	5	7	9
Total	40	100	80	100

1 USD = 22,200 Mozambican Metical (2004 Monthly average)

Consistent with the findings from the 2005 SAMP survey, the migrants stay away from home for long periods and return home only for short annual vacations. In the average year, the migrant spends 10-11 months a year away from home and only rarely visits during that time. Around three-quarters said they see their partner just once a year or even less frequently. Some 17% said the last visit was more than a year ago. Only 24% had seen their partners in recent weeks.

SWAZILAND SURVEY FINDINGS

The reality of HIV and AIDS is well-recognized by both migrant mineworkers and rural partners. Both groups said that more people were dying in the home area than in previous years. Some indicated that almost every weekend there were funerals; others that funerals were often conducted simultaneously because of the number of deaths. A quarter of the respondents cited AIDS as the leading cause of death of miners and ex-miners. Others cited occupational injury (22%), tuberculosis (19%) and other disease (19%). Only 2% cited witchcraft and hunger. AIDS also stands out as the leading perceived cause of death of community members in general (31%). Other causes of death mentioned included TB (20%), other diseases (21%), witchcraft (5%), heart attacks (4%) and old age (4%).

A 2003 Survey concluded that "Swazi people are highly knowledgeable about HIV/AIDS/STIs but this knowledge has not translated into desirable behavioural change."[45] This study made a similar finding. All respondents were very aware of HIV and AIDS. The majority of both migrants (68%) and rural female partners (67%) said they were aware that AIDS is not curable. Most also disagreed with common myths that a person can get infected through sharing a meal with an infected person, sharing tools at work, sharing a bed, sharing clothes or shaking hands. Reasonably high levels of awareness about protection were also demonstrated. Abstinence was viewed by over 60% of migrants and partners as a main means of protection, which may have to do with messages preached by the churches in Swaziland.

However, interesting differences about the efficacy of condoms emerged between the two target groups (Figure 5). While over 80% of rural women saw condoms as an effective form of protection, the proportion of men was much lower (at 43%). While 20% of women said that avoiding blood transfusions was important, hardly any men mentioned transfusions. On the other hand, nearly 10% of the miners saw the protection of traditional healers as a viable means of prevention. Women appear to have much less faith in traditional healers' remedies. None cited this as a viable means of protection.

Figure 5: Main Means of Protection Against HIV

Avoid sharing razor blades
Seek protection from traditional healers
Avoid blood transfusion
Avoid sex with prostitutes
Limit number of sex partners
Limit sex to one partner
Use condom
Abstain from sex
Partners
Miners
0 10 20 30 40 50 60 70 80 90
Percentage

Note: More than one answer permitted.

Self-assessment of risk showed that more women than men felt they were at risk of HIV infection (Figure 6). Nearly 80% of miners felt that they were at low or no risk at all and only 15% thought they were at high risk. Most workers who said they were at low risk noted that it was because they were faithful to their partners, even though the responses to other questions contradicted this assertion. Those who said they were at high risk blamed their partners: they felt that they could not trust their partners and believed they were unfaithful.

Figure 6: Self-Assessment of Risk of Infection

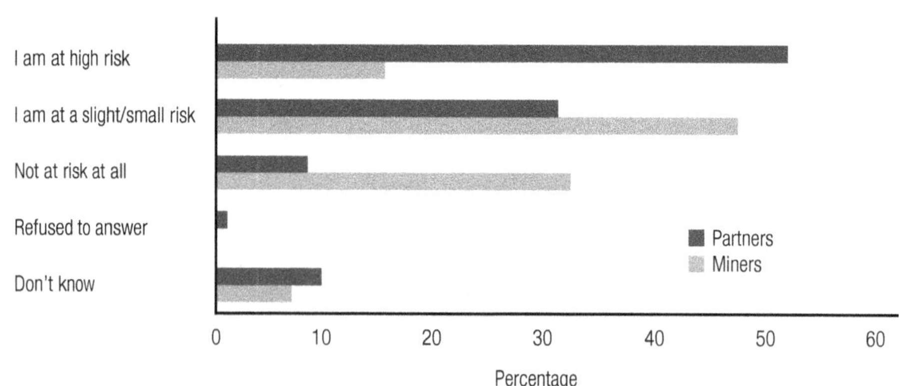

In dramatic contrast, rural partners were much more pessimistic about their risk of infection. Over half (51%) felt that they were at high risk and only 8% said there was no risk at all. Women's sense of vulnerability came from the perceived behaviour of their partners, not their own. Most of the women who felt they were at high risk felt this way because their partners engaged in high-risk sex with others. Nearly half (48%) said their migrant partners were not faithful and/or did not want to use condoms. Another 22% said that they were at risk because they had no idea about their partners' sexual activity while away from home. A further 12% said they did not trust their partner. In other words, over 80% of the women who said they were at high risk blamed their migrant partners for their own vulnerability. If the migrants are to be believed, these fears are groundless. The lack of trust amongst miners and partners dominate the feelings of those who consider themselves at high risk and raises important concerns about the psychological stresses that migration puts on inter-personal relationships.

In light of the fundamentally different risk perceptions of mine migrants and rural women and the apparently high levels of mistrust between them, the survey sought to gain some insights into actual risk taking behaviour. The migrants exhibited a strong inclination for multiple sexual partnerships (Figure 7). Only 7% said they had had only one lifetime partner. Another 30% said they had had sex with between 2 and 5 women and 33% with between 6 and 10 women. Twenty two percent had had more than 10 partners. These findings are not inconsistent with other studies of the sexual practices of migrant miners in Southern Africa.[46] In sharp contrast, 35% of female partners said they had had one lifetime sexual partner and a further 32% only two. Just 14% said they had 5 or more partners and only 3% had had 10 or more. The women said that having multiple partners is not that common in rural areas.

The primary anomaly is that migrant miners do not generally view themselves as a high risk group, yet have multiple sexual partners. Given their awareness of HIV and AIDS, this might imply that they take adequate precautionary measures. Such a hypothesis should, at the very least, translate into high levels of condom use. In fact, nearly three quarters of those who had had sex in the previous 30 days had not used a condom. Asked why, the majority responded either that they did not like them (37%), had forgotten to use them (20%) or did not think they were necessary (17%) (Figure 8). In general, however, these migrant miners do not appear to have a good sense of the heightened risk of having unprotected sex with multiple partners.

Figure 7: Number of Lifetime Sexual Partners

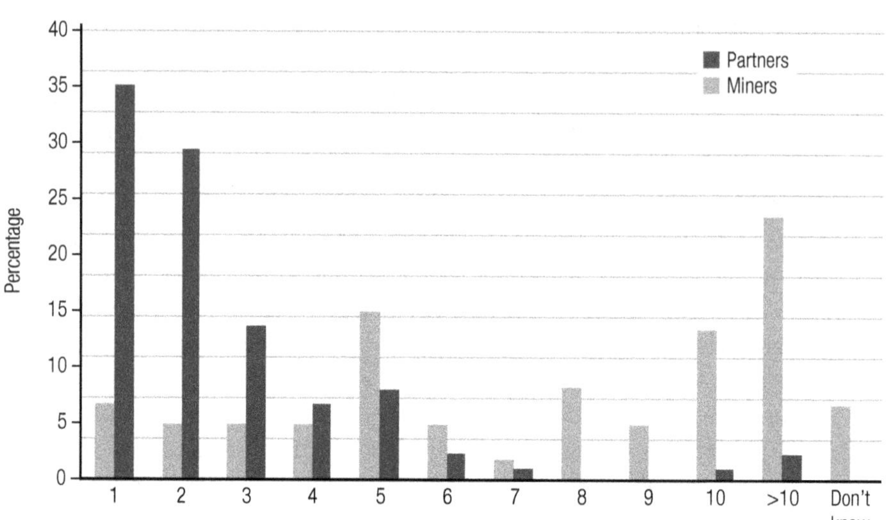

Figure 8: Reason for Not Using Condom During Last Sexual Act

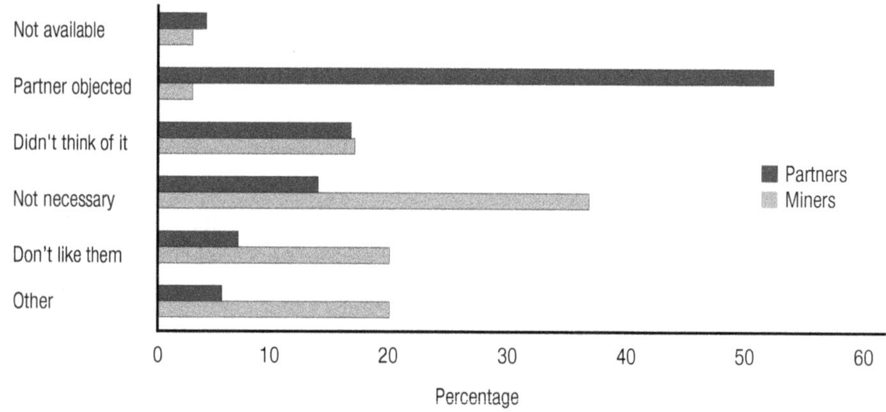

A different pattern emerges with rural partners. Condom use is as low as that of the male migrants: 79% had not used a condom during their last sexual act. However, unlike their male counterparts, this had very little to do with a dislike of condoms (only 14% versus 37% of men), though some did forget (6%) or think it unnecessary (17%). What is most striking is that 53% did not use condoms because their partners objected to their use. In other words, while rural partners in mine-sending areas protect themselves through limiting the number of sexual partners, this does not render them invulnerable to infection because condom use is so low. This increased vulnerability is rooted in gender relations of inequality with partners who reject condom use while simultaneously engaging in high risk sexual behaviour themselves at the mines.

Unequal gender relations, the relative lack of power of women, women's status and gender-based violence have all been advanced to explain the vulnerability of migrant and non-migrant women in Swaziland.[47] UNDP's gender analysis of the Swaziland epidemic concluded:

> Women's vulnerability to HIV infection is increased by economic, social and cultural factors and by different forms of violence (particularly sexual), that place them at a disadvantage within relationships, the family, the economy and society at large. Women's economic dependence on men, their high poverty levels and lack of access to opportunities and resources, contribute to their vulnerability to HIV infection. Because of the economic dependence on men, women are unable to take control of their lives and protect themselves against HIV infection.[48]

The report also observes that women in Swaziland are expected by men to be subordinate and submissive, that it is considered acceptable for men to have multiple sexual partners, and that certain practices (such as polygamy, arranged marriage, widow inheritance and the reed dance) all contribute to the spread of HIV. The vulnerability of women is explicitly acknowledged by the Swaziland government.[49] However, "there is no legislation in place to protect the basic rights of women."[50] In other words, while migrancy puts many Swazi men at risk, it is gender relations within Swaziland that heightens the vulnerability of most women. When high-risk male migration is combined with gender inequality in migrant-sending areas, the risk for women, particularly spouses and partners (regular and casual), is magnified. If women were empowered to make their own decisions about sexual behaviour and protection, the impact of high-risk behaviour by migrant men would be accordingly reduced.

MOZAMBIQUE SURVEY FINDINGS

Knowledge of the existence of HIV and AIDS is reasonably high amongst Mozambican miners. However, as many as 60% thought that AIDS was curable. Of these, 22% claimed that modern medicine held a cure and 15% cited traditional medicine. A higher proportion of rural partners know that AIDS is incurable (61% compared to 40% of miners). Knowledge that unprotected sex was the major means of transmission was also far from universal (60% of miners, again lower than the rural partners at 69%) (Figure 9). Knowledge of the importance of using condoms as protection against HIV was higher (Figure 10).

In theory, given the existence of HIV and AIDS education programmes on the mines, miners ought to be better informed about HIV and AIDS than their Mozambican partners. In fact, rural women were slightly better informed about the risks. Nearly 30% of women saw fidelity as a means of protection compared with only 12% of men. However, a third of the men said that avoiding sex with commercial sex workers was important, which indicates some awareness of the risks associated with transactional sex.

Figure 9: Perceived Methods of Contracting HIV/AIDS

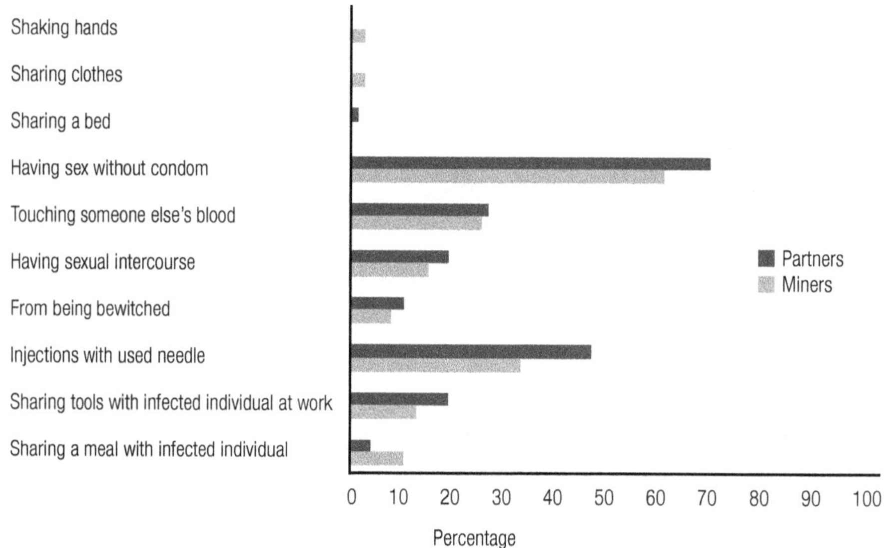

Figure 10: Means of Protection from HIV

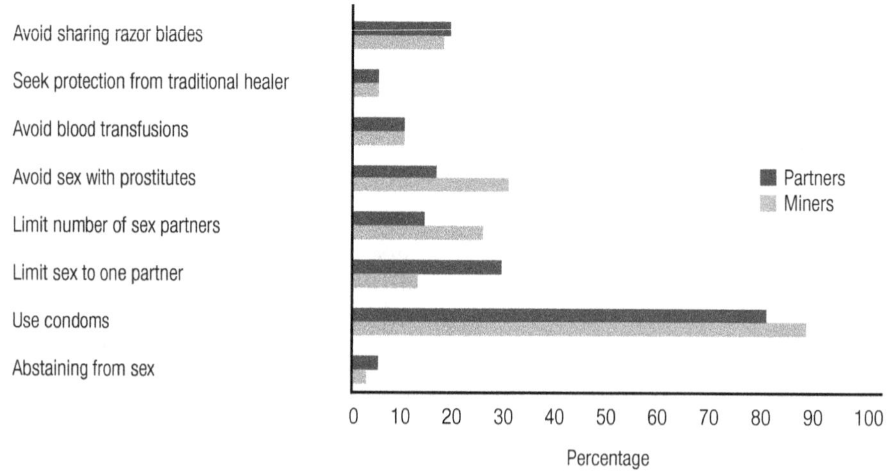

When asked to identify the symptoms associated with HIV and AIDS, there were distinct differences between the levels of knowledge and understanding exhibited by miners and rural partners. Less than a third of the miners were able to identify any symptoms associated with HIV and AIDS. The symptoms identified by the others were non-specific and could reflect almost any common disease: cough, loss of weight or appetite and fever. The rural partners fared somewhat better on this question although as many as half admitted they did not know any of the symptoms of HIV and AIDS. The most commonly listed symptoms listed by the partners were diarrhea, skin boils or lesions, weight loss, recurrent vomiting and hair loss. Many of the spouses listed multiple symptoms, often three or more per respondent. The distinction between miners and their spouses is dramatic and may be because residents of Chokwe are far more likely to encounter people with AIDS on a daily basis.[51]

AIDS was cited as the major cause of mortality in the home districts by rural partners (Figure 11). Personal exposure to people with AIDS is clearly a factor in raising awareness and understanding of HIV and AIDS. Only a small number of miners admitted having a close friend living with HIV and AIDS, and only one said they knew of a close relative with the disease. Only a quarter of the miners acknowledged that they knew someone with AIDS. More of the partners knew someone living with HIV and AIDS. They were more likely to know of a close relative with the disease than a close friend. Nine percent had a close friend, and 13% had a close relative, with HIV or AIDS.

Figure 11: Main Causes of Death in Home Communities (Partners)

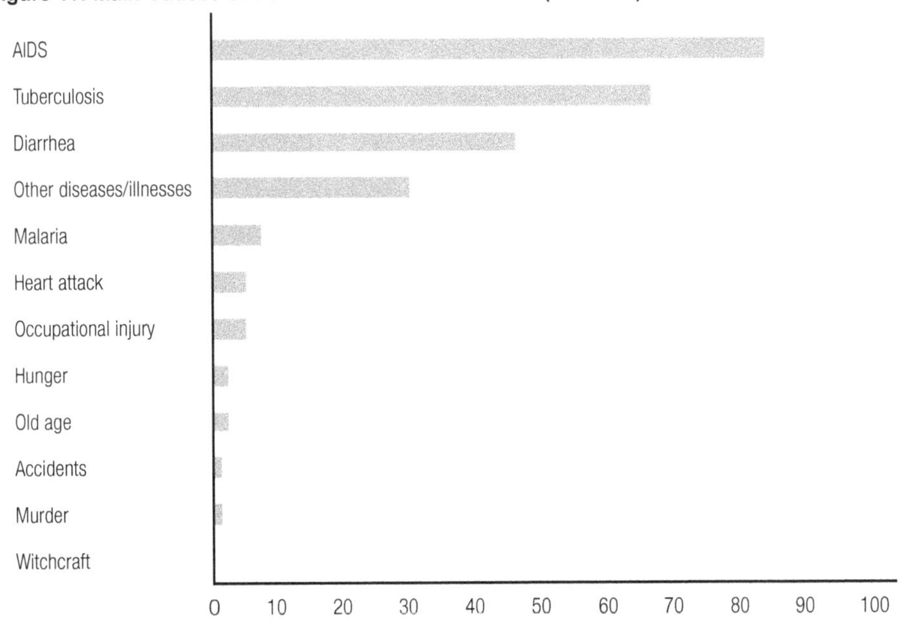

Most (90%) miners said that they felt that HIV and AIDS was a problem at the mines and that they worry about the disease a lot. Three-quarters felt they were at high risk of becoming infected and only three of the respondents felt they were not at risk. At the same time, not all miners had taken active measures to ascertain their own status. Less than a third of the miners had ever been tested for HIV (30%) and just over half of those (17% of total) had voluntarily sought testing. The vast majority of the female partners also said they worry about HIV/AIDS a lot (93%) and 94% agreed that it was a problem in the community. Three-quarters felt that they are at high risk of becoming infected with the disease. Only one individual felt she was at no risk at all. Yet, few partners had actually sought out an HIV test; only 16% of the women had been tested, all voluntarily.

The pursuit of a stable and enduring relationship is extremely difficult under circumstances of prolonged separation. All of those interviewed reported having at least one sexual partner in their lifetime, and many reported multiple partners. All but one of the miners said they were currently sexually active, not all with regular partners. Nearly 40% of the miners said they had engaged in sexual relations with someone who was not their spouse or primary partner in the previous 12 months. Forty three percent of this group said they had had sex with women who requested money or goods in exchange. The frequency of these encounters ranged from once to six times per year.

Despite the fact that the majority of both miners and partners view themselves as at risk of contracting HIV and know that condom use is the primary means of protection, actual use of condoms is sporadic and low. None of the miners said they always or almost always used a condom during sex. Even those that did use condoms did not use them every time they have sex. One miner said he had used a condom only once during the previous month and yet had 10 sexual encounters with his regular partner. Another had used a condom for only 4 of his 22 encounters during the last month. When asked why they did not use condoms all the time, the largest number (38%) said they did not like them, while 25% said that they simply forgot. Another 15% did not think condom use was necessary. None of the miners said that access or cost was a deterrent to using condoms (Table 8).

In other words, most Mozambican miners are at risk, know they are at risk, know how to reduce the risk, yet do not take precautions to reduce that risk. This paradox has been pointed out by previous researchers.[52] Condoms are freely available and their efficacy is recognized. Yet there is clearly not a culture of condom use amongst miners. The stated reasons given for non-use relate primarily to personal taste and forgetfulness. Campbell also concluded that migrant mine workers display "continued commitment to a macho notion of masculinity that undermined the likelihood of condom use...Several miners commented that the condoms provided by the mines could not be trusted because they were of a poor quality and had often passed their 'use by' dates. Some suggested that it was these very condoms that were causing the HIV infection."[53]

Table 7: Reasons for Not Using Condoms

	No.	%
Not available	0	0
Too expensive	0	0
Partner objected	3	7.5
Don't like them	15	37.5
Used another form of contraceptive	3	7.5
Didn't think it was necessary	6	15
Didn't think about it	9	22.5
Other	1	2.5

Note: Multiple responses were allowed

As argued above, the infrequency of home return of Mozambican miners considerably reduces the risk that rural partners will contract the virus from their HIV positive migrant spouses or partners. That risk would be reduced still further if miners acted on their belief in the protective value of condoms when having sexual relations with their partners at home. All the miners interviewed said they engage in sexual activities with their regular partners. However, the majority reported not using condoms with their partners. Most miners (80%) had not used a condom at all with their regular partner at any point in the previous year. Sixty five percent said they had not used condoms with their regular partner over the past month. None of the miners said they always or almost always use a condom with their partners.

The responses of rural partners confirmed this finding. None of the women had used a condom for every sexual encounter in the previous year and only 8% said they had used condoms every time they had intercourse. Fifty five percent said they had not used condoms at all over the previous year. Eighty-five percent of the women who had sex in the month prior to the interview had not used a condom. When asked about low condom use, just under half (46%) responded that their partners objected to condom use. A further 10% said that they did not want their partners to think they were infected with HIV. Approximately half of the respondents said they would have chosen to use condoms but did not feel they had that option. Those that did use them did so sporadically. Usage is low primarily because female partners lack the power to effectively negotiate condom use.

By their own admission, many of the partners of Mozambican mine migrants have other relationships when their partners are away at the mines. Given the fact that most rural women rarely see their migrant partners, the potential for other relationships to develop is high. Nearly one in five respondents said they had sex during this period with someone who was not their primary partner or spouse and where no financial transaction took place. In addition, women are highly dependent on the remittances sent home by their partners. As such, they remain very vulnerable to the remitting behaviour of their partner. If the remittances are irregular or insufficient, household poverty deepens. Resorting to selling sex for cash or goods is a not uncommon response. In the twelve months prior to the interview, 14% admitted having had sex in exchange for goods or money.

Of the 46 women who admitted having sexual relationships other than with their regular partner (57% of the total sample), just over 35% gave sexual satisfaction and emotional support as the primary reason while another 33% cited financial reasons and support for children (Figure 12). Condom use was no more consistent with non-regular partners, suggesting that women's power to negotiate safe sex is no stronger with casual than regular partners. The responses of partners in rural Mozambique suggest that vulnerability in the mine-sending areas is not simply a function of the exposure of female partners to HIV through returning migrant partners.

Figure 12: Women's Reasons for Having Other Partners

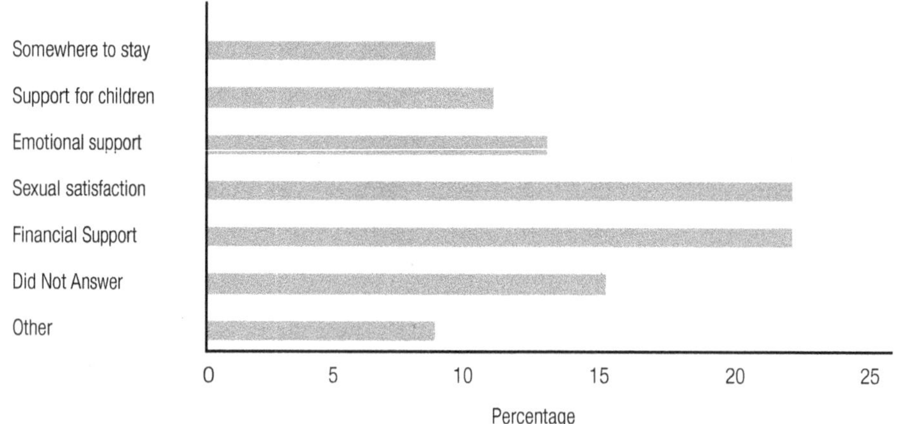

Conclusion

Collins argues that "donors [and others] have ignored a key structural reason why HIV continues to spread in Mozambique – and elsewhere in Southern Africa – today: the continuation of the region-wide, low-wage migrant labour system. This system continues to fragment family life, thus helping sustain Mozambique's – and Southern Africa's – HIV pandemic. If donors and African governments are serious about stemming the rising tide of HIV, they must begin to explore long-term alternatives to this migrant labour system – and to the dominant export-led development model on which this system is premised."[54] The findings of this study support the relevance of Collins' observation and confirm that rural migrant-sending areas have become high-risk zones for HIV infection for women.

Migrant miners are long-term, career workers. As long as their health holds and their mine does not close, they keep their jobs. Age and experience do not appear to have had any significant mitigating impact on their high risk behavior. While the evidence collected here relies on self-reporting, many miners not only have additional regular partners when they are at work but frequent contact with commercial sex-workers at hotspots around the mines. The impact of extended separation and the high-risk living and working environment that has always characterized the mines, continues to facilitate, if not encourage, high-risk behaviours that greatly increase the chances of HIV infection.

Knowledge of HIV and AIDS is reasonably good amongst residents of these two traditional mine migrant-sending areas in Swaziland and Mozambique. Many of the common myths about HIV are held by only a tiny minority. Most seem to know what puts them at risk, know that the disease is fatal, know that ART is not a remedy and do not appear to have a great deal of faith in traditional healers. One exception is the rather large proportion of Mozambican miners who believe the disease is curable. If anything, rural partners are better informed than miners which must say something about the efficacy of mine education programmes. In both Mozambique and Swaziland, the main source of knowledge is not workplace programmes on the mines or in the community nor peer education nor the medical community, but radio. This could be seen as an additional indictment of conventional workplace and community-based education programmes. On the other hand, it demonstrates the critical importance and potential of radio as the medium for education.

Perception of personal vulnerability is high. Yet, both miners and female rural partners of migrants appear to place themselves at risk through their behaviour. The reasons are, however, quite different. In the case of miners at work, high risk behaviour is a consequence of the migrant labour system which sees them spend the greater part of the working year away from home in an all-male environment of macho masculinity with easy access to transactional sex.[55] These miners certainly know that condom use would reduce their risk of contracting HIV but actual use is sporadic to non-existent. Condom use is rejected on grounds of personal preference or attributed to forgetfulness.

Condom use does not seem to be a very effective means of reducing risk in rural sending areas either as condom use is low there. Miners at home are even less likely to use condoms than when on the mine. This does not appear to be related to unavailability. None of the informants mentioned this as an obstacle to use. The risks of contracting HIV are certainly lower (since commercial sex workers on the mines exhibit much higher HIV prevalence than rural partners). But their very unwillingness to use protection puts their rural partners at greatly increased risk.

While migrant men give "pragmatic" reasons related to sexual pleasure, necessity and forgetfulness, rural partners' answers are lodged in the dynamics of gender inequality. Women's lack of use of condoms has virtually nothing to do with personal preference. Partners of migrant miners wish to use condoms. Their inability to do so with the frequency and consistency that they would like is related to the preferences and demands of men. Any woman who insists on condom use is seen to be implicitly questioning her partner's fidelity. Miners clearly expect their partners to be faithful and do not see themselves at risk when they go home. This combination makes regular and consistent condom use extremely unlikely as women lack the power to insist on condom use. Ultimately, therefore, it is the gendered relations of inequality that make it very difficult for women to protect themselves.

One interesting contrast is that Mozambican miners recognize that they are at high risk of infection while Swazi miners do not. Three quarters of Mozambican miners thought they were at "high risk" of infection compared to only 15% of Swazi miners. Since, by any objective criterion, they are, in fact, equally vulnerable, the real question is why so many Swazi miners underestimate the risk. If Swazi mine workers consistently used condoms, and Mozambican miners did not, this might explain the different perceptions of vulnerability. Yet the two groups of miners were equally uncommitted to regular and consistent condom use. While only a few did not use them at all, none of the miners used condoms every time they had sexual intercourse. Over 80% of Mozambican miners believe that condoms were an effective form of protection against HIV, compared with only 40% of Swazi miners. Yet the latter did not give this as a reason for not using condoms. The reasons given by both groups were familiar, and not unlike the reasons that men generally in this region give for not using condoms: they simply did not like them (nearly 40% of both

Mozambicans and Swazis), they forget (25% of Mozambicans and 28% of Swazis) or they really do not think they are necessary (17% of Swazis and 17% of Mozambicans).

One of the basic hypotheses of this study is that different migration patterns affect the risk profile of miners and rural partners. Mozambican miners return home only once a year for annual leave. Swazi miners, in contrast, visit home at least once a month or every month or two. Yet, as far as these studies could ascertain, both engage in equally risky behaviour while they are away at work. Frequency of return home therefore does not appear to have any mitigating influence on the sexual practices of mineworkers at work. What it clearly does do is to place Swazi women at greater risk than their Mozambican counterparts.

The comparison between Mozambican and Swazi women suggests that the Mozambican partners may be more prone to forming other relationships outside their primary relationship for a host of different reasons including emotional and financial support. One study has shown that many Mozambican migrants form longer-term attachments at the place of work, even to the point of establishing second households with South African women.[56] In some cases, increased poverty from a reduced flow of remittances (because of the demands of a second household in South Africa) may force rural women to seek support through other relationships. However, most Mozambican migrants are forced to defer 60% of their pay to Mozambique, a policy that enjoys almost universal support amongst the partners of migrants.[57]

A final common feature that emerged in this study between Mozambique and Swaziland, by both men and women, is the low level of personal knowledge of HIV status. This is clearly a conscious choice since testing is available and accessible to all. The reasons for the reluctance to be tested require further investigation. However, it is doubtful that even if the rates of knowledge of status were increased it would lead to higher rates of disclosure. Clearly, considerable stigma still surrounds the disease. Miners and partners are largely uninterested in knowing their status and in disclosing it to others, especially to their own partners and families.

This study has confirmed that mobility and vulnerability are intimately connected. It has also suggested that the causes and consequences of vulnerability of migrants and their partners are closely connected. The primary objective was not to reconfirm much of what we already know about the vulnerability of migrant miners at work but to examine the perceptions and attitudes of the rural partners of miners and, thereby, to shed more light than currently exists on the vulnerability profile of women in migrant-sending areas.

ENDNOTES

1 C. Evian, M. Fox, W. MacLeod, S. Slotow and S. Rosen, "Prevalence of HIV in Workforces in Southern Africa, 2000-2001" *South African Medical Journal* 94 (2004): 125-30.

2 K. Jochelson, M. Mothibeli and J. Leger, "Human Immunodeficiency Virus and Migrant Labor in South Africa" *International Journal of Health Services* 21 (1991): 157-73.

3 E. Gouws and Q. Abdool Karim, "HIV Infection in South Africa: The Evolving Epidemic" In S. Abdool Karim and Q. Abdool Karim, Eds, *HIV/ AIDS in South Africa* (Cambridge: Cambridge University Press, 2005), p. 60.

4 J. Glynn, J. Murray, A. Bester, G. Nelson, S. Shearer and P. Sonnenberg, "Effects of Duration of HIV Infection and Secondary Tuberculosis Transmission on Tuberculosis Incidence in the South African Gold Mines" *AIDS* 22 (2008): 1859-67; S. Basu, D. Stuckler, G. Gonsalves and M. Lurie, "The Production of Consumption: Addressing the Impact of Mineral Mining on Tuberculosis in Southern Africa" *Globalization and Health* 5:11 (2009).

5 J. Hargrove, "Migration, Mines and Mores: The HIV Epidemic in Southern Africa" *South African Journal of Science* 104(1&2) (2008): 53-61.

6 C. Campbell, *Letting Them Die: Why HIV/AIDS Prevention Programmes Often Fail* (London: James Currey, 2003); C. Campbell, "Migrancy, Masculine Identities and AIDS: The Psychosocial Context of HIV Transmission on the South African Gold Mines" In E. Kalipeni, S. Craddock, J. Oppong and J. Ghosh, eds. *HIV & AIDS in Africa: Beyond Epidemiology* (Oxford: Blackwell, 2004), pp. 144-54; B. Williams, D. Taljaard, C. M. Campbell, E. Gouws, L. Ndhlovu, J. Van Dam, M. Carael and B. Auvert, "Changing Patterns of Knowledge, Reported Behaviour and Sexually Transmitted Infections in a South African Gold Mining Community" *AIDS* 17 (2003): 2099-2117.

7 R. Packard, *White Plague, Black Labor: Tuberculosis and the Political Economy of Health and Disease in South Africa* (Berkeley: UC Press, 1989); E. Katz, *The White Death: Silicosis on the Witwatersrand Gold Mines, 1886-1910* (Johannesburg: Witwatersrand University Press, 1994); K. Jochelson, *The Colour of Disease: Syphilis and Racism in South Africa, 1880-1950* (Oxford: Palgrave, 2001); S. Marks, "The Silent Scourge? Silicosis, Respiratory Disease and Gold Mining in South Africa" *Journal of Ethnic and Migration Studies* 32 (4) (2006): 569-89.

8 S. Marks, "An Epidemic Waiting to Happen? The Spread of HIV/AIDS in South Africa in Social and Historical Perspective" *African Studies* 61 (2002): 13-26.

9 A. Dladla, C. Hiner, E. Qwana and M. Lurie, "Speaking to Rural Women: The Sexual Partnerships of Rural South African Women whose Partners are Migrants" *Society inTransition* 32(1) (2001).

10 C. Collins, "Mozambique's HIV/AIDS Pandemic: Grappling with Apartheid's

Legacy" UNRISD Programme on Social Policy and Development, Paper No. 24, 2006, p. 5.

11 K. Macarow, "Transmission Routes: The Global AIDS Epidemic in South Africa and France" *Global South* 2(2) (2008): 92-111.

12 M. Lurie, B. Williams, K. Zuma, D. Mkaya-Mwamburi, G. Garnett, M. Sweat, J. Gittelsohn and S. Abdool Karim, "Who Infects Whom? HIV-1 Concordance and Discordance Among Migrant and Non-Migrant Couples in South Africa" *AIDS* 17(15) (2003): 2245-52; M. Lurie, B. Williams, K. Zuma, D. Mkaya-Mwamburi, G. Garnett, A. W. Sturm, M. Sweat, J. Gittelsohn and S. Abdool Karim, "The Impact of Migration on HIV-1 Transmission: A Study of Migrant and Non-Migrant Men, and Their Partners" *Sexually Transmitted Diseases* 40 (2003): 149-56; K. Zuma, M. Lurie, B. Williams, D. Mkaya-Mwamburi, G. Garnett, A. Sturm, "Risk Factors of Sexually-Transmitted Infections among Migrant and Non-Migrant Sexual Partnerships from Rural South Africa" *Epidemiology and Infection* 133 (2005): 421-8.

13 B. Auvert et al, "HIV Infection Among Youth in a South African Mining Town is Associated with Herpes Simplex Virus-2 Seropositivity and Sexual Behaviour" *AIDS* 15 (2001): 885-98; R. Gray et al, "Probability of HIV-1 Transmission Per Coital Act in Monogamous, Heterosexual, HIV-1 Discordant Couples in Rakai, Uganda" *The Lancet* 357 (2001): 1149-53; S-G Mahiane et al, "Transmission Probabilities of HIV and Herpes Simplex Virus Type 2, Effect of Male Circumcision and Interaction: A Longitudinal Study in a Township of South Africa" *AIDS* 23 (2009): 377-83; M-C Boily et al, "Heterosexual Risk of HIV-1 Infection Per Sexual Act: A Systematic Review and Meta-Analysis of Observational Studies" *The Lancet* 9(2) (2009):118-129; W. Miller, N. Rosenberg, S. Rutstein and K. Powers, "Role of Acute and Early HIV Infection in the Sexual Transmission of HIV" *Current Opinion in HIV & AIDS* 5(4) (2010): 277-82.

14 M. Coffee, M. Lurie and G. Garnett, "Modelling the Impact of Migration on the HIV Epidemic in South Africa" *AIDS* 21(3) (2007): 343-50.

15 J. Crush, S. Peberdy and V. Williams, "International Migration and the Southern African Region" Report for Global Commission on International Migration (GCIM), Geneva, 2004.

16 J. Crush, *The Struggle for Swazi Labour, 1890-1920* (Montreal and Kingston: McGill Queens Press, 1989); P. Harries, *Work, Culture, and Identity: Migrant Laborers in Mozambique and South Africa, c. 1860-1910* (Portsmouth NH: Heinemann, 1994).

17 F. de Vletter, *Sons of Mozambique: Mozambican Miners and Post-Apartheid South Africa*, SAMP Migration Policy Series No. 8, Cape Town, 1998.

18 Swaziland Vulnerability Assessment Committee (VAC), "A Study to Determine the Links between HIV/AIDS, Current Demographic Status and Livelihoods in Rural Swaziland" (Mbabane, 2004).

19 Ministry of Health and Social Welfare, Swaziland, 9th Round of National HIV

Sero-surveillance in women attending antenatal care services at health facilities in Swaziland. Survey report, 2005.

20 A. Whiteside, C. Andrade, L. Arrehag, S. Dlamini, T. Ginindza and A. Parikh, "The Socio-Economic Impact of HIV/AIDS in Swaziland" Report for HEARD, Durban, 2006.

21 A. Whiteside, "What Is Driving the HIV/AIDS Epidemic in Swaziland and What More Can We Do About It?" Report for NERCHA and UNAIDS, Mbabane, 2003, p.32.

22 Ibid.

23 Ibid, p. 8.

24 J. Crush, B. Williams, E. Gouws and M. Lurie, "Migration and HIV/AIDS in South Africa" *Development Southern Africa* 22 (2005): 293-318.

25 Whiteside, "What Is Driving the HIV/AIDS Epidemic in Swaziland," p. 33.

26 Campbell, *Letting Them Die*.

27 Whiteside, "What Is Driving the HIV/AIDS Epidemic in Swaziland," p. 12.

28 F. Muwanga, Impact of HIV/AIDS on Agriculture and the Private Sector in Swaziland (Mbabane: TAT Health Services, 2002), p. 26.

29 Central Statistical Office, *Report on the 1997 Population Census* (Mbabane, 1998).

30 Collins, "Mozambique's HIV/AIDS Pandemic," p. 2.

31 R. Waterhouse, "The Impact of HIV/AIDS on Farmers' Knowledge of Seed: Case study of Chokwe District, Gaza Province, Mozambique" Research Report of the International Crops Research Institute for the Semi-Arid Tropics, 2004, p. 7.

32 C. Arndt, "HIV/AIDS, Human Capital and Economic Prospects for Mozambique" Africa Region Working Paper Series No. 48, World Bank, Washington, p. 39.

33 K. Foreit, A. Barreto, P. Noya and I. Nhatavf, "Population Movements and the Spread of HIV/AIDS in Mozambique" *Journal of Health and Human Services Administration* 24 (2001): 279-94.

34 S. Beckmann and P. Rai, *Mozambique: HIV/AIDS, Work and Development* (Geneva: ILO, 2005), p. 4

35 F. de Graca Bukali, "HIV/AIDS Prevention and Care in Mozambique, A Socio-Cultural Approach" UNESCO, Maputo, 2002, p. 17.

36 Beckman and Rai, Mozambique.

37 Ibid, p. 12.

38 R. First, *Black Gold: The Mozambican Miner, Proletarian and Peasant* (London: Palgrave Macmillan, 1983).

39 de Vletter, *Sons of Mozambique*.

40 F. de Vletter, "Labour Migration to South Africa: The Lifeblood for Southern Mozambique", in *On Borders: Perspectives on International Migration in Southern Africa*, D McDonald, Ed, (Cape Town and New York: SAMP and St Martin's Press, 2000), pp. 46-70.

41 Waterhouse, "The Impact of HIV/AIDS on Farmers' Knowledge of Seed," p. 12.
42 H. Simelane and J. Crush, *Swaziland Moves: Perceptions and Patterns of Modern Migration*, SAMP Migration Policy Series No 32, Cape Town, 2004.
43 Emalangeni, equivalent to ZAR.
44 F. de Vletter, *Migration and Development in Mozambique: Poverty, Inequality and Survival*, SAMP Migration Policy Series No 43, Cape Town, 2006.
45 Whiteside, "What Is Driving the HIV/AIDS Epidemic in Swaziland," p. 22.
46 Campbell, *Letting Them Die*.
47 B. Tobias, "A Descriptive Study of the Cultutal Mores and Beliefs Towards HIV/AIDS in Swaziland, Southern Africa" *International Journal for the Advancement of Counselling* 23 (2001): 99-113; A. Buseh, L. Glass and B. McElmurry, "Cultural and Gender Issues Related to HIV/AIDS Prevention in Rural Swaziland" *Health Care for Women International* 23 (2002): 173-84; UNDP, "Gender Focused Responses to HIV/AIDS. The Needs of Women Infected With and Affected by HIV/AIDS," Mbabane, 2002; H. Simelane, "Husbands, Wives and Domestic Violence in Post-Colonial Swaziland" unpublished report, University of Swaziland, 2006.
48 UNDP, "Gender Focused Responses," p. 1.
49 Government of Swaziland, "Policy Document on HIV/AIDS and STD Prevention and Control" Mbabane, 1998; Government of Swaziland, "Swaziland National Strategic Plan for HIV/AIDS 2000-2005," Mbabane, 2000.
50 S. Gumedze, *HIV/AIDS and Human Rights in Swaziland* (Pretoria: Centre for the Study of AIDS, 2004), p. 24.
51 P. McKenzie, "Chokwe: Dying on its Feet", *Ottawa Citizen*,Thursday, August 10, 2006.
52 Campbell, Mzaidume and Williams, "Gender as an Obstacle to Condom Use"; C. MacPhail, and C. Campbell, "I Think Condoms are Good But, Aai, I Hate Those Things: Condom Use Among Adolescents and Young People in a Southern African Township" *Social Science and Medicine* 52 (2001): 1613-27.
53 Campbell, *Letting Them Die*, p. 156.
54 Collins, "Mozambique's HIV/AIDS Pandemic," p. 1.
55 Campbell, *Letting Them Die*.
56 S. Lubkemann, "Migratory Coping in Wartime Mozambique: An Anthropology of Violence and Displacement in 'Fragmented Wars'" *Journal of Peace Research* 42 (4) (2005): 493-508.
57 de Vletter, *Sons of Mozambique*.

MIGRATION POLICY SERIES

1. *Covert Operations: Clandestine Migration, Temporary Work and Immigration Policy in South Africa* (1997) ISBN 1-874864-51-9
2. *Riding the Tiger: Lesotho Miners and Permanent Residence in South Africa* (1997) ISBN 1-874864-52-7
3. *International Migration, Immigrant Entrepreneurs and South Africa's Small Enterprise Economy* (1997) ISBN 1-874864-62-4
4. *Silenced by Nation Building: African Immigrants and Language Policy in the New South Africa* (1998) ISBN 1-874864-64-0
5. *Left Out in the Cold? Housing and Immigration in the New South Africa* (1998) ISBN 1-874864-68-3
6. *Trading Places: Cross-Border Traders and the South African Informal Sector* (1998) ISBN 1-874864-71-3
7. *Challenging Xenophobia: Myth and Realities about Cross-Border Migration in Southern Africa* (1998) ISBN 1-874864-70-5
8. *Sons of Mozambique: Mozambican Miners and Post-Apartheid South Africa* (1998) ISBN 1-874864-78-0
9. *Women on the Move: Gender and Cross-Border Migration to South Africa* (1998) ISBN 1-874864-82-9.
10. *Namibians on South Africa: Attitudes Towards Cross-Border Migration and Immigration Policy* (1998) ISBN 1-874864-84-5.
11. *Building Skills: Cross-Border Migrants and the South African Construction Industry* (1999) ISBN 1-874864-84-5
12. *Immigration & Education: International Students at South African Universities and Technikons* (1999) ISBN 1-874864-89-6
13. *The Lives and Times of African Immigrants in Post-Apartheid South Africa* (1999) ISBN 1-874864-91-8
14. *Still Waiting for the Barbarians: South African Attitudes to Immigrants and Immigration* (1999) ISBN 1-874864-91-8
15. *Undermining Labour: Migrancy and Sub-contracting in the South African Gold Mining Industry* (1999) ISBN 1-874864-91-8
16. *Borderline Farming: Foreign Migrants in South African Commercial Agriculture* (2000) ISBN 1-874864-97-7
17. *Writing Xenophobia: Immigration and the Press in Post-Apartheid South Africa* (2000) ISBN 1-919798-01-3
18. *Losing Our Minds: Skills Migration and the South African Brain Drain* (2000) ISBN 1-919798-03-x
19. *Botswana: Migration Perspectives and Prospects* (2000) ISBN 1-919798-04-8

20. *The Brain Gain: Skilled Migrants and Immigration Policy in Post-Apartheid South Africa* (2000) ISBN 1-919798-14-5
21. *Cross-Border Raiding and Community Conflict in the Lesotho-South African Border Zone* (2001) ISBN 1-919798-16-1
22. *Immigration, Xenophobia and Human Rights in South Africa* (2001) ISBN 1-919798-30-7
23. *Gender and the Brain Drain from South Africa* (2001) ISBN 1-919798-35-8
24. *Spaces of Vulnerability: Migration and HIV/AIDS in South Africa* (2002) ISBN 1-919798-38-2
25. *Zimbabweans Who Move: Perspectives on International Migration in Zimbabwe* (2002) ISBN 1-919798-40-4
26. *The Border Within: The Future of the Lesotho-South African International Boundary* (2002) ISBN 1-919798-41-2
27. *Mobile Namibia: Migration Trends and Attitudes* (2002) ISBN 1-919798-44-7
28. *Changing Attitudes to Immigration and Refugee Policy in Botswana* (2003) ISBN 1-919798-47-1
29. *The New Brain Drain from Zimbabwe* (2003) ISBN 1-919798-48-X
30. *Regionalizing Xenophobia? Citizen Attitudes to Immigration and Refugee Policy in Southern Africa* (2004) ISBN 1-919798-53-6
31. *Migration, Sexuality and HIV/AIDS in Rural South Africa* (2004) ISBN 1-919798-63-3
32. *Swaziland Moves: Perceptions and Patterns of Modern Migration* (2004) ISBN 1-919798-67-6
33. *HIV/AIDS and Children's Migration in Southern Africa* (2004) ISBN 1-919798-70-6
34. *Medical Leave: The Exodus of Health Professionals from Zimbabwe* (2005) ISBN 1-919798-74-9
35. *Degrees of Uncertainty: Students and the Brain Drain in Southern Africa* (2005) ISBN 1-919798-84-6
36. *Restless Minds: South African Students and the Brain Drain* (2005) ISBN 1-919798-82-X
37. *Understanding Press Coverage of Cross-Border Migration in Southern Africa since 2000* (2005) ISBN 1-919798-91-9
38. *Northern Gateway: Cross-Border Migration Between Namibia and Angola* (2005) ISBN 1-919798-92-7
39. *Early Departures: The Emigration Potential of Zimbabwean Students* (2005) ISBN 1-919798-99-4
40. *Migration and Domestic Workers: Worlds of Work, Health and Mobility in Johannesburg* (2005) ISBN 1-920118-02-0

41. *The Quality of Migration Services Delivery in South Africa* (2005) ISBN 1-920118-03-9
42. *States of Vulnerability: The Future Brain Drain of Talent to South Africa* (2006) ISBN 1-920118-07-1
43. *Migration and Development in Mozambique: Poverty, Inequality and Survival* (2006) ISBN 1-920118-10-1
44. *Migration, Remittances and Development in Southern Africa* (2006) ISBN 1-920118-15-2
45. *Medical Recruiting: The Case of South African Health Care Professionals* (2007) ISBN 1-920118-47-0
46. *Voices From the Margins: Migrant Women's Experiences in Southern Africa* (2007) ISBN 1-920118-50-0
47. *The Haemorrhage of Health Professionals From South Africa: Medical Opinions* (2007) ISBN 978-1-920118-63-1
48. *The Quality of Immigration and Citizenship Services in Namibia* (2008) ISBN 978-1-920118-67-9
49. *Gender, Migration and Remittances in Southern Africa* (2008) ISBN 978-1-920118-70-9
50. *The Perfect Storm: The Realities of Xenophobia in Contemporary South Africa* (2008) ISBN 978-1-920118-71-6
51. *Migrant Remittances and Household Survival in Zimbabwe* (2009) ISBN 978-1-920118-92-1 2009
52. *Migration, Remittances and 'Development' in Lesotho* (2010) ISBN 978-1-920409-26-5